Without a Witness

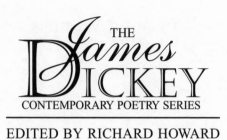

THE
James
DICKEY
CONTEMPORARY POETRY SERIES

EDITED BY RICHARD HOWARD

Without a Witness

Poems by
Stella Johnston

UNIVERSITY OF SOUTH CAROLINA PRESS

Published in Columbia, South Carolina, by the
University of South Carolina Press

Manufactured in the United States of America

04   03   02   01   00   5   4   3   2   1

Library of Congress Cataloging-in-Publication Data

Johnston, Stella, 1959–
    Without a witness : poems / by Stella Johnston.
       p.   cm. — (The James Dickey contemporary poetry series)
       ISBN 1-57003-342-0 (alk. paper) — ISBN 1-57003-343-9 (pbk. : alk. paper)
      I. Title.   II. Series.
    PS3560.O386455 W58   2000
    811'.6—dc21   00-010793

Acknowledgment is made to the editors of the following publications, where some
of the poems included here first appeared, sometimes in slightly different form:
New Republic, "Nuclear Medicine"; *Paris Review,* "Julian"; *Shenandoah,* "Andro-
meda" and "Ball Lightning: Palestine, Texas, 1952"; *Western Humanities Review,*
"The Clown Doll" and "Telling Stories."

NATIONAL
ENDOWMENT
FOR THE ARTS

Publication of this book was supported by a grant from the National
Endowment for the Arts.

*For my mother
and for Jerry and Nathan*

Gardeners, come,
come here and ponder
a Rose that, when cut,
lives all the longer.

Sor Juana Ines de la Cruz, *The First Dream*

Contents

A Note on Stella Johnston   xi

I

New World   3
Of Being Alive   5
Water Music   9
Andromeda   13
For J. B. Smith, Alive or Dead   15

II

"The Hanging Tree"   21
De Natura   23
Composition   26

III

Ball Lightning: Palestine, Texas, 1952   31
Not a Step   34
The Clown Doll   37
Nuclear Medicine   39
Celebrating More Than 100 Years of Aluminum   40

IV

Julian   45
War Stories: Memorial Day, 1989   48
The Loa Loa   51
Telling Stories   53

A Note on Stella Johnston

Now give me a drink of water. Here's
to all that's done but still unfinished.

Take my hand. The Gods can never die.

Poets seem to discover their own forms, their own formalities—the kind
that really help them say what they mean to say, rather than the ones
learned or loaned (these lapse), usually in the course of a considerable ini-
tiation period, during which the trials and tactics of the art may be appre-
hended or, more likely, be warded off. It is extraordinary to me that Stella
Johnston arrived at, actually *landed on,* the necessary diction of her dra-
matic lyrics from the very start, without the usual huffing and puffing that
characterize the tyro in matters of verse, that ceremony of returns. Her
speech is, as I say, dramatic, which means it is also distilled. Take any
handful of lines, such as these from "Ball Lightning":

There's someone standing in an open door.
There's a sickly smell of sulfur

and back in the kitchen, a kettle's
boiling over on the stove.

It's morning.
When nothing else can happen, the rain begins.

And it appears, it *resonates,* that there is a certain density, even a *manteia*
about the words and the way their edges meet. Her language, that is to say,
has passed through the stage of being rhetoric, and has come out into the

light and darkness of revelation, an unveiling indeed. Only a couple of the poems are specifically about her own somatic disasters, though more concern the sequels and backwashes of such disorder:

We are in a dark room together,
myself and my breathing machine.

I am lying on my back
when the doctor's shape moves in.

I press the usual questions.
Today, in this room without a witness,

he answers:
"Your father's dead and you'll never walk again."

Even when she mythologizes her experience, as in "Andromeda" or "Of Being Alive," what beguiles Johnston most is aftermath, consequence, actually *survival.*

The mysteries of how the new poet (and none I know of is so new as Johnston, taking the brilliant air like a morpho butterfly just out of its cocoon, wings still damp and not yet rid of their creases of constraint) compels her utterance leave me wondering on the threshold of her poems, entering and leaving and quite happy to be there.

This is the authority, these are the accents of Marina, daughter of Pericles rescued from shipwreck, "given by one that had some power." Her poems begin often enough in Texas, but they end—rather they do not end, but echo ever after—in the territory of *legend,* what must be read, as *memoranda* must be remembered, as *delenda* must be destroyed.

RICHARD HOWARD

I

New World

In Church's "Twilight
in the Wilderness" God
is light. He
oozes through the red-orange air,
into each indentation of land, between the grasses,
all around the weather-beaten aspens, the world, in fact,
opposite. My grandmother's century: the twilight

requires this moving shadow. It is as if
God finds Himself only while looking
everywhere for us,
which is why His countenance creeps forward,
lonely and sad. A large bird
meets the approaching sun
turned sideways atop a tree.
Within the hour
all of these will disappear
at the spectrum's touch: manifest,

the pond at the painting's bottommost cleft
will unveil its scummy edges,
the color-heavy layers of cloud recede.
By that time, a wood frame house might emerge

from the darkest foreground,
its door wide open, a woman's figure moving around inside,
sweeping, her broom sending puffs of dirt
across the worn stoop

across the porch
and into the landscape

in open contradiction to the artist's wish
to give us "dreamy Nature with folded hands"
in the last few moments before dawn.

Of Being Alive

Whenever I see him he is always falling
like a dancer caught in mid-leap
by invisible wires
behind a dark, dark, gauzy scrim.

The world in which he's falling
is one of gravities, pressures,
a vast amniotic enclosure,
a false surface

that is the real vision, the one
no picture can show you.
He'll never land anywhere,
never crumple on the lunar surface,

his mouth open upward to where
the light went away
as sediments older than any country
settle over his pajamas. Plain. Flannel.

Hard to describe the pattern. Worn
around the edges. Drifting like that,
fathomless,
the distance in my mind.

*   *   *

I have prowled the blackest waters
like a fish that feels its way instead of sees it.

I have seen the rust's accretion
make the hull into a kind of cave.

He woke me up, put my heavy coat
over my nightgown
and dragged me up the stairs.

I wanted to go back, my doll, I cried,
he said, hush now, there isn't time
and I wailed all the way into the water.
I don't know, I never will know
what he was doing,
waving, maybe blowing me a kiss.

After seventy-three years
just imagine how it is for me to see
her head, her very own head, gone completely bald,
smiling in the primeval mud
eyeless and green but somehow still staring
out of the page in *National Geographic*
as if at the girl I once was . . . :

to her right an electric heater from a first-class cabin,
to her left a champagne bottle, unopened.

*　　*　　*

There is a story about two Norwegian fishermen, brothers,
who slip into a maelstrom.
The funnel's wall is smooth as blown glass.
With an almost sickly fascination

the younger one makes a study
of the wreckage he is part of:
above him, a swirl of sky and clouds,
the deafening vortex below.

The solid and more bulky configurations
tend to be pulled down fast
while the light, hollow shapes stay where they are
so he calls out "Let go of the mast and come with me!"

In a choice dictated by survival
he then decides to do what he must.
We always do exactly what we must.
Alone, in complete comprehension,

he sees their revolutions growing smaller
so he takes a deep breath
jumps from the sinking deck
and grabs a barrel.

                *   *   *

We barely moved. The few
puffs of cloud barely moved.
The water wore a glassine finish.

It might have been a postcard
except for one thing,
the object at the vanishing point

where the circumferences gathered.
It moved then to break itself in half.
The scream was indescribable
and only slightly human.

It tore
apart the nighttime by its seams.
You could hear the groaning of a giant door:
come in, come in, come in.

Followed by a little gasp, it closed
after which the silence filled up
each and every space inside it.

The tow was just a ripple
by the time it arrived. It rocked
us softly up and down once:

the circle stitched itself shut.

Water Music

This is supposed to be an after-death experience,
one of the warm, floating variety,
moving through a long dark corridor
toward the light.

There is supposed to be an ancestral vision.
The dead should be waiting: Irish, English, German—
all leveled down to the immortal nationality of love.
They are going to tell

the secrets passed down to them by God himself.
They are going to reveal the meaning
behind suffering, ecstasy, death.
Loved ones are supposed to be

opening their arms on the other side in welcome.
Their fingers should be in reach of mine,
generous and lovely, like the touch
of God's hand on the roof

of the Sistine Chapel. There is supposed to be
anything but what these intent strangers see
before them: a dead girl
who's been tossed

around like a Raggedy Ann in a dryer
then brought here, all but broken in half.

This girl is not transcendent. No,
she is practically buried already.

*   *   *

*I open my eyes. I have not been watching myself
from the ceiling. I have very simply opened*

*up my eyes and looked up, the only
available direction from where I lie.*

*Everyone here is extremely excited, as though
they are somehow afraid of my still-aliveness,*

*evidenced only by a glance from my not-dead eyes.
A male voice has proclaimed the need to remove my clothing*

*with scissors. His tone indicates the need to be in a hurry.
I am not in a hurry. I have more time than I've ever had in my life.*

*I am thinking about blue jeans going into the trash can
in a white room filled with white light in the middle of West Texas.*

*   *   *

If you'd ever been given large doses
of morphine, then you would know
how it is that a piece of rhythmical breathing
equipment can become

a seven-foot wooden puppet that lowers
one arm to strike you on the neck
at regular intervals. You would know how
a dream can take

hold and repeat itself without ever reaching
a conclusion. They won't allow real water,
real Coke, real liquid anything
and when she cries

about how thirsty she is, they tell her
that the I.V. is keeping her hydrated and offer
her lemon swabs to suck and ice chips, one
at a time, to dissolve

in her mouth. The dream takes root.
It comes in pieces. Smooth rocks, hot beneath her feet,
keep her moving through the bed
of a great river. She is

deep in the bottom of a narrow canyon. She is
to suffer an enlightenment. In fact, she sees it already.
It's been there, waiting, so large
it fills the entire gorge

from wall to wall and she knows
without seeing beyond it that it isn't
strong enough to hold
the water back

and that she will die when it breaks,
that the dam is wrong and that the river is right,
that she has to die so that
the river might live.

*   *   *

We are in a dark room together,
myself and my breathing machine.

I am lying on my back
when the doctor's shape moves in.

I press the usual questions.
Today, in this room without a witness,

he answers:
"Your father's dead and you'll never walk again."

Andromeda

Nowadays, my husband looks the other way
when I leave to take a long walk again
into the island's hills outside our walls.
It's there I can feel the held breath of rock,
a cool forgetfulness under my feet.
He thought that would do it, taking off her head!

That day, chained, all I could think was how,
when the serpent tore me from the cliff, my hands
might have stayed. There they would have been,
twisting like poppies out of metal sleeves.
That's why I cried, why I couldn't speak.
He thought it was modesty. He was in love

and stood there, hero: supple, strong, his hand
unflinching on the hilt of his sword.
he said his own desire was to set me free.
I've never told him, impossible, how that day,
day of his victory, I couldn't help but look
across his shoulder right into eyes come up

from beneath a veil of ocean to be slaked
on me. My husband flew but I was seen
and somehow claimed. Strange that I blush
among thoughts whispered to no one, not even
the pretty slave girl who is sometimes sent
to fetch me to the house. She announces,

"Lady, your presence is requested."
Then she's gone like the quick orange crabs on the beach.
Wailing for their sister, two immortals
thrashed an island senseless with their wings.
Mighty Perseus cut her down in her sleep.
Perhaps her body rooted fast, drank deeply

of the salted ground and grew. Shadow-blossoms,
who could guess what shade your stems unfurled?
I remember twisted trees, a wind . . .
It was an ugly place that shuddered, stark
as Cimmeria, or Lethe's drafty banks.
Husband, you're a synonym for brave, with Hermes

at heel, Athena on your breast and in your hands.
Contend, gods demand, and make you think
it's possible to win. But agate-eyed Medusa
is nothing you carry off like a trophy.
Stone to flesh, flesh to stone, there's more
than can be undone, even by the son of a god.

"Zeus came to Danae in a shower of golden rain."
That's how the story always starts: his birth.
He's home right now telling it all again
to another listing herd of wet glass rings.
Sooner or later, I'll be walking in.
I am Andromeda, his lovely bride

whose curls fall back against the marriage bed
so tenderly for him, when we writhe.
Alone, I close my eyes: there's something else
between my face and its damp image, a life
that could disappear as I could disappear
in a loneliness that's neither land nor sea.

For J. B. Smith, Alive or Dead

Homer might have told you
he's the only real loser in the whole *Odyssey*.
I'm talking about that sad sack, that milquetoast among icons,
Elpenor, who wasn't "terribly powerful in fighting

nor sound in his thoughts."
Somehow he made it through Troy.
It was during the long intermission on Circe's island,
at the bon voyage party, after a whole

year of feasting—a warrior ought to get
anxious, all that wine and lying around in the yard
with enchanted animals—but the thought of months,
maybe years at sea, the hoisting and hauling,

staring over the edge of the swift black ship,
oars splashing across the wine-dark sea,
no reflection anywhere, up or down,
such an eerie sameness that even the soul

becomes monotonous, constrained . . .
The spirit has to have somewhere to go, after all,
when it doesn't fit in. Why be torn away from pleasure?
Why not drag it out a little longer,

one with the night to walk out into the night
beneath a sky full of stars, then to seek a way up.
I can see him as he takes hold of stones,
finding footholds, scaling an imaginary mast.

He's made it to the roof of Circe's palace
and now he's chatting with Olympus.
Indeed, he reminds me of you
the very last time I saw you

somehow maneuvering upright
long past that magical number of drinks
when a normal human would have passed out.
Across the sunken dance floor I was spotted.

You started waving, *I'm coming over. Great,* I smiled,
nodding back, but you didn't walk around;
instead, you opted for the shortcut,
through the slam dancers jumping like pistons

under the tilting ceiling grid of lights.
Pulled to the floor by an undertow of arms and legs,
even then you came on,
like a buoy in a hurricane,

stupidly impossible to drown
while one song mixed into another,
some wise-assed rapturous refrain
mindlessly repeated for a good beat,

Don't you want me baby, don't you want me?
I watched you, sitting and not thinking,
I could say thinking and not being,
nearly "gone" as it was, as it sometimes can be

when the insides of the skull,
a gallon thing, begin to waver,
and the mind, immersed in glassy fluids,
rolls, withdraws, refocuses

the way things are to fit the heart's must-be:
so sad and serious and comic. You did make it
all the way to me. You knelt down
where I sat and breathed hard into my ear:

"You have a special place in my heart."
Your eyes actually pleaded with mine. Before long,
I wanted you to leave me alone
but instead I let you babble endlessly

and sincerely on the same way Elpenor did
when his journeying comrades arrived
at the kingdom of the dead. He *still*
could not remember how it was at dawn,

that, "when his companions stirred to go, he,
hearing the tumult of their talking,
started suddenly up, and never thought,
when he went down, to go by way

of the long ladder, but blundered
straight off the edge of the roof
so that his neck bone was broken out of its sockets
and his soul went down. . . ."

He was pacing the other bank of the river
when they bumped against land.
All that time, he had been waiting
to see the familiar faces of his friends.

Upon Odysseus and the others
he poured out his heart until it was empty.
Then he kneeled beside the dread water,
cupped his hands together and drank.

II

"The Hanging Tree"

The past is making everybody suffer.
There's the past you can't remember,
the past you remember too well

and the past that belongs to somebody
you maybe want to love
as if your own past was not enough

as if together, finally and forever,
we could make up a whole new past
that leads right up to this moment—

but it isn't yours, it isn't even theirs,
credits scrolling down
like Revelation's list of the saved

across a grisly icon, clawed and black
against Technicolor red. Moments ago,
Gary Cooper was there,

hands bound behind him,
sitting on a horse, his neck in the noose,
his face a stony mask of resignation.

We all know the territory—and what
could be more "western" than a hanging
in the heart of the mythical badlands

where justice arrives at the courthouse
too late or not at all and dreams
come to scorn the ones who dreamed them;

there's never room for love in this vast unknowing.
Someone always dies before it's over
and along with what the saddlebags will carry,

the hero rides away . . . and how we treasure
his loneliness, the loping gate to nowhere,
the sad harmonica under the starry sky.

So here's the problem presented by this story:
Gary Cooper lives, saved by a woman
who struck gold. She buys off the bloodthirsty mob

by giving them all she has: the deed
to her "grub stake" called "The Lucky Lady."
Defying genre, she removes the noose

and the twosome ride off screen together.
The rope hangs, empty and abandoned,
more a part of the tree than anything else

as a lone guitar joins some violins
and the screen seemingly zooms away
into the distance, more and more separate.

De Natura

Two scientists, Penzias and Wilson,
wanted to make the final, bottom-line adjustments
on their brand new radio-wave-measuring machine
so they aimed it precisely

into one after another
of the best-known spaces in space
but they couldn't find nothing.
Something kept on interfering,

denying their sensitive zero,
buzzing with a fly-from-millions-of-light-years-away
tiny buzz. It was
to say the least, an enormous discovery,

that out there everywhere you look,
traveling a distance immeasurable by anything but sound
the merest spectral disturbance
is heading our way,

falling all over and around every bit of who we are,
melting into our rooftops, our hair, and leaving behind
its invisible layer of ashes.
One night years ago, I stayed awake

until the sun came on like an interrogator's lamp,
all to the purpose of composing a poem,

(due the next day) in which I imagined
all of my friends at that moment, sailing

over vast oceans of sleep
while I tipped my ear toward Pythagorus' universal music.
All night, I studied the back-beat cacophony
in the heating system's on and off hiss

and the bluesy refrigerator's low bursts of humming
as it gently cooled its insides. The poem was a total loss,
but I am still here, years later,
seduced by the same kinds of things.

Brought up on the Baptist Church
and science fiction, my soul
craves life support, weightlessness, distance . . .
There's nothing new underneath the sun,

just the anarchy of elements.
Nevertheless, as Krishna reminds
the warrior Arjuna just before facing
the destruction of the world,

the soul keeps asking its usual questions,
if time really passes and how did we get here,
drinking yet another cup of tea
from the bright red mug with a porcupine on it

while the Romulans keep on scheming on Channel 29.
The cup of tea, like Arjuna, is meant to be empty.
His job is not to know, but to listen.
But whose voice whispers like static

along the lines that blaze gently inward,
scything out hopelessness, clearing a new garden

where Adam and Eve are no longer content
with their meager diet of knowledge,

redundant now anyway, since
they've done and known everything,
heard and seen everything, even God
scribbled out on graph paper,

refusing not to exist
while two tired scientists
hunch over their damnable machine's
feeble annunciation, mute and unbroken.

Composition

Last night I dreamed I'd changed
with soft, furry, angular, how can I say this: *female* arms,
a large, crudely puckered mouth

that gasped, involuntarily,
and a hulking, jerky body. Still somewhat human,
I lacked wings. My husband

stood beside me in the laboratory,
much taller and leaner than himself. Together
we were strangely undistressed.

Our very first behavior
was brutally and shamelessly to couple
on the laboratory floor after which we were

informed by the presiding mad scientist
that "that's just the way flies act."
I was awakened by a sharp pain, a hunger,

frisked the comforter
and went right back to sleep.
I was in the very same country

only this time I was forcing my way
down a pathway through a jungle.
Something had to be finished

in a desperate hurry. There was also
an acute impression of having failed.
After all, there I was,

having suffered all that way
only to arrive at last in a thatched hut
where a nurse in a starched white uniform

smoothed my fingers one at a time
across a steel table. She told me,
"Never forget to keep your nails clipped."

III

Ball Lightning: Palestine, Texas, 1952

One filling station is open on Highway 19: a seance
of yellow pumps under a horizontal lamp. All night long

trucks have been driving past in their usual headlong fury
making the sound of an ugly, anonymous complaint

dragged out mile after mile, ". . . wrong . . . wrong . . ."
Inside the station on a bulletin board a smudged

map of the state looks like it's just about to fall
from its tacks. Like all good maps this one succeeds

at a calm connection of all it contains. Lines, dots:
synapse, cell: like the brain of a mystic lost

in meditation, poised on the verge of renouncing the world,
the map is both humble mirror and full explanation.

The young attendant is asleep at the desk on a centerfold.
His half-open mouth has made a little dark pool

on the thigh of a shapely brunette. The brunette's
mouth is open too. Her eyes are passionately fixed

on the oily ceiling. The tip of her tongue
is extended: an invitation, a ready wick . . . although

the truth of course is that she's every bit as blind, flat
as the side panel on an orange tractor where dawn,

a little ways off, is beginning to break: an edge
of orange mist. There's a woman standing in a yard.

She's watching a storm move in from the west,
a line of dark clouds. When the wind picks up

her chintz house coat flaps like the loose corner
of a sail against the backs of her legs. The cloth,

thin from years of washing, lies smoothly pressed
around the curve of her stomach. Her breasts seem to pull

her forward, two heavy lobes, as, motionless,
her whole body listens. When the bolt

arrives it's right into the top of the mimosa,
the new pink fans suddenly transfigured

into veins of light that flare into brief points
and eclipse. Then, as if from out of the dying tree

they appear, maybe a half dozen glowing spheres,
six yellow-violet suns moving about three feet above

the ground, surfaces wormy with light.
She reaches out to one that's come up close

and pulls her hand out, slowly trailing
one blue resonant cord of flame . . .

There's someone standing in an open door.
There's a sickly smell of sulfur

and back in the kitchen, a kettle's
boiling over on the stove.
It's morning.
When nothing else can happen, the rain begins.

Not a Step

I dreamed that Andy Warhol
had a mansion with a basement torture chamber.
Gigantic portraits of soup cans lined the walls
around the racks, wheels, pots of boiling oil,

and so on. A more than matronly
bookkeeper stepped out of her office—this place
had an office—arriving just in time to say,
"Wait. We made a mistake with this one."

She drove me out under the Hollywood stars
in a limousine, my silver-coifed tyrant
throwing me a leer that meant, "Whoever you are,
I nearly had you." Well, something nearly did

have me once. I would tell you how
over the litter of a windshield, the sky
opened up, vaginal and transpierced with light,
and how a man stepped in just before me,

taking my hand and leading me toward
a distant singing, the absolute joy
I felt moving closer, *at last,* then
how he turned and ordered me back,

releasing my hand into the darkness of
my waiting corpse but I can't. I don't recall a vision.

So there I am having lunch with a friend
who's just come back from a retreat with Ram

Dass. The guru's eyes were a clear blue
that made him think of Christ. He lays down his fork
and tells me about traveling
out of his body. "Everything is ours!"

His hand knocks against the wall as he sweeps
out a circle of how much that is.
My friend says he's not afraid to die.
Death, the guru told him, is nothing more

than taking off a shoe that doesn't fit.
Ah, but haven't I been there before, that place
looks familiar, this flesh is too tight.
See, the still-to-come keeps adding up until

it's a garment so invisible and large
that only a missing person would ever wear it.
Meanwhile, those drunken suitors are downstairs
eating you out of house and home, I mean,

those private disappointments. They're lonely.
They want to get married. Which is how
the story gets longer and longer . . .
It's the Marquis de Sade

in his well-furnished cell at the Bastille
scratching sheets of parchment
nearly marginless with tiny black words.
Like nature, this man is relentless.

Even the seasons go by, a slow movement
from left to right in the cell of his skull.

Today, his passion's universal. He ponders
the ultimate crime: *to snatch the sun*

from out of the sky, to make a general darkness
and to use that star to burn the world!
But the prison is about to be stormed.
Quickly, they load up his things, promising

to rescue the book, but the book,
his precious book: the punishments, the lists of rules,
the beautiful children, the cooks, the faithful wives,
the hidden chateau, the ancient whores

whose job is to render the narratives
night after night—the whole book
is left behind and for all he'll ever know
it was burned out of being, up into

that accidental heaven where nothing's
extraordinary, nothing's ugly. Poor Alphonse,
listen, your manuscript survived! I
have read it! And if it could somehow speak

between its own lines it would want you
to know that your pain is its jurisdiction.
Father, bigger than life, and out of my reach,
your loss was a lie. Mine is the glory of art

which means committing your fatal mistakes
over and over. The vision is always personal,
always historic, and there's not a single word
that doesn't take you farther down.

The Clown Doll

I held him and slept with him.
He returned my love with nothing
but a deep softness of body,
an undying cheerfulness of face.

If there was ever any sorrow in him
it was only what I gave
of my own supply. Defiantly joyous,
he suffered

my spankings, my apologies, my talks,
as if to please me was
his whole life until one day
in a hiding place I built outside

with a thrown-away blanket
and a couple of old chairs,
inside, where I'd put him
along with a cigar box full of yarn

and the *Book of Spells*
from which I'd meant to chant,
for luck, perhaps,
or love, with a candle I set a fire,

it was an accident, flames rising so fast
there was only time enough to escape.

I ran in numbly through the back door
toward my mother shouting "Fire . . .

fire . . ." in the dark, the spikes of light
already high enough
to cause some neighbor to call
a truck. My mother switched the backs

of my thighs with a long, pliant
limb off the fig tree. I didn't
cry. That night as I fought
myself to sleep again and again

I saw him catching fire. He was sitting
up watching the yellow flame
consume, first, his red hands and feet
then up red and white striped legs, arms,

his white cotton rectangular torso
darkening under a painless burst of heat,
the sudden torch of his body
joined to the box of yarn, the tent, the world

from which I had departed forever.
Still smiling, obscenely happy,
his rubbery face ignited, grew larger
then collapsed into the tarrish lump

I found days later
among cold blackened sticks in the dirt
when I was brave enough to look,
to find out what he'd actually become.

Nuclear Medicine

Is that my kidney and my swarming bones?
I wonder, could they pick me up in Russia,
all isotope, as the narrator concludes,
". . . her marrow no longer behaves abnormally."
Applause. More X-ray than all of you combined,

from here it's hard to tell one glow from the next.
Enough to be the centerpiece on this slab
where the mechanism's auto-driven eye
whirrs and pierces, semicircular, overhead.
"Set me up: I could take down missiles."

Suddenly wanting very much to say,
"Hey, you missed the best part of the story . . ."
But white coats merge until they disappear
down tiled hallways of you're-still-here
and the gray-green screen is coming up empty.

Celebrating More Than
100 Years of Aluminum

What do you think of a metal as white as silver, as unalterable as gold, as easily melted as copper, as tough as iron; which is malleable, ductile, and with the singular quality of being lighter than glass?

Charles Dickens, Household Words

The end of the world as we know it
should have come, as Nostradamus is supposed to have said,
in 1999, or there's always the Revelation version:
"No man shall know the hour of His coming."
At any rate, we've landed

on more than a few of those new worlds already,
times when it seemed like life itself
was being yanked out from under our feet,
no signs of transfiguration, no burning bushes,
only an ache in the pit of the chest

where something irreplaceable is gone,
gone forever. Who wouldn't long for the last great annulment
who has already known the occasional clench
of an inward hand—its deathly squeeze,
and it gets all mixed up with love, too,

these breathless moments of piercing through
to whatever has never been trusted,
that seems to survive. Even at nine,

I could think of myself as the mighty Quetzal in flight.
I hugged those enormous stones all the way up

to the top of the Pyramid of the Sun
where I stretched my arms skyward
and gave myself over. Then, in a while,
bored with the god, I lay down and played
sacrifice. When the long knife opened my chest

my heart looked exactly as helpless and small
as the sparrow I once buried in the back yard.
I remembered the station wagon parked
near the place where idols were for sale.
Fear spoke words to me then.

It said, "Stand up, silly, you're all alone
and look, they're waving you down."
More of the same gods and goddesses
grimaced and stuck out their tongues at us
on the Aztec floor of the Museo Archeologico.

A sudden violence conquered my mother's body,
no doubt from the water, so we had to leave,
but not before I heard the guide saying how
this enormous sandstone thing, the holy wheel of time,
runs out in either 1986 or two thousand something,

depending on how one reads the dizzying
rounds of encrypted numbers. It does
live with us still, one out of many futures,
full, coming up around us like blood-red moons,
urging us on while the penchant for calamity

stays with the rotting seeds in the naked ground,
the ones we ought to feel sorry for,

that never make it up, and we should all
be so lucky. Then again, there are those among us—
remember Napoleon—who learn

to read what is left in the sad remains
of the overthrown, who keep for themselves
the knowledge of how the world
can change all at once in our sleep,
that being one of the fortunate means

to wake up to the dream's desire
when it first appears, unbelievably light.
The emperor presented a rattle to his baby boy
molded with soft-edged angels: his way of announcing
a new curiosity to the court. There they are

at a long table, lifting burnished forks
to their parted lips, against the grain of a metal
more precious than gold, its gleam in the candlelight lovely
and dull and even more fresh than the arabesque
woven into a young lady's bodice

who is laughing so hard
that burgundy can be traced all the way
from the corner of her mouth to a pool between her breasts.
Her uncle, the baron, just made an ungentlemanly sound
then at once his face said "Oh!" and his eyebrows went up!

IV

Julian

For Richard Howard

My beloved Helios is leaving. See
how the hem of his robe slips from the tent
as Chaos' daughter approaches, such
sublime generosity from which they lend
proportion to our world: and it is
our world, Maximum, never theirs who
would call it a mere dominion, our days
but work, our nights but simple sleep,
our lives but weary prologue to the most
dismal eternity ever imagined. I gave
them more Sisyphus than they wanted,
though, didn't I, when I took our temples

back. When they wept and complained I
reminded them of how their own gospels
teach them to bear suffering with patience
like their own pacific martyr. These
two years since Constantius' deadly fever,
we've seen the old altars uncovered. No
crackers, sips of wine, delicate gesturing
over embroidered silk but cattle, goats, sheep,
the thrusted ritual blade, the naked stone
surface overflowing with blood. The priests
called it a disgusting mess. I called it
the grandeur of the human soul in immortal

union with divine love and sent the meat
out to the poor. But you, dearest friend,
of all people understand the spirit's
hunger. "If the Greek is stirred by art,
the Egyptian by an animal, or another
by a river or a fire, let each," you said,
"Behold God's essence in what is beautiful
in the world." Who else could have convinced
Constantius' dogs not to murder me, but
to send me into exile, and where else
but to the very groves that once heard
Plato's voice. You took me to Eleusis.

When I finally came up, my face
streaked, my mouth and fingers stained the red
of pomegranates, you gave me barley-water
flavored with mint and said, "Drink
always from the cup of sorrow and remember
what we are." Tell me now, Maximus, what
am I if not the happiest of men? But
you must see to yourself. There are
no more vicious beasts than Christians.
Jovian, you know, will succeed me and the grave
theologians are going to hang their sallow,
watered-down Osiris up everywhere they can.

They would take death herself away
from nature. Why, just imagine a deity
who would think his own children lucky
to be shut into a garden, the one thing
that lends order to the human mind
dangling there deliciously before them,
vibrant with promise, along with another
that, once partaken of, would make them
equal to himself, tell them *eat of all
else but these two,* and then, finally,

when, teased beyond belief, they disobey,
blame it on a snake! But Helios is calling:

my light must be added. Down invisible stairs
the fire travels until all is radiance,
even the homeliest of things. Take this
javelin, for instance. Look how worn
the grip, how ground away the point
from being sharpened over and over
before battle, how washed out its Persian
decorations. How far from its maker it
has come only to reveal so little of itself.
How naturally it darkens with my blood.
Now give me a drink of water. Here's
to all that's done but still unfinished.

Take my hand. The Gods can never die.

War Stories: Memorial Day, 1989

In Hermann Park in Houston, Texas
the crowd wavers mirage-like past the edge
of live-oak shelter we inhabit, puffing

the heated air. My baby wants
to nurse himself to sleep; the woman
reclined on a portable lawn chaise

who shares our shade drinks from a can
in a paper bag and sings along
with something only she can hear

through the headphones of her walkman.
The Allies are making preparations:
some nearby Scotties warming up their pipes,

Yanks and Tommies gesturing back
and forth between the howitzer
and the zone of Germans nested

on the hill with a machine gun
on the backside of the amphitheater.
How could I help but think about

my war-hating, English-teacher father.
The Battle of the Bulge in the middle
of a Texas heat wave would have provided

irony enough for one sarcasm after another;
these men displayed for our amusement,
not stone cold and buried in their foxholes.

He would have pointed out how some things
are not meant—no, cannot be—reenacted
and he knew *that* war's elements well enough—

"dropped" as they say in the midst of island jungle
to bestow literacy on "interrogations"—he wrote reports,
wearing the same thick, black-framed glasses

from OSS training unit pictures that he has on
in front of the English building at Columbia,
beside *The Thinker.* He just doesn't fit

among such remote aspects of harm
as machine gun fire, malaria and starvation,
his head full of poems by Keats and Whitman,

sweating over a notebook, holding a pen,
the Romantic doing the work of the homicidal.
So it's true he never recovered: neither did they—

shot in the back, I'm told, after they had spilled their guts,
believing their freedom bought for information.
The fluent Japanese I never heard him speak

must be what lived so fitfully inside him,
pronunciations startling him in his sleep so that
he cried out sometimes incoherently at night,

waking up everyone. And to think that we call
this other place a theater . . . For the moment,
Major Albert Sidney Johnston, Jr.'s grandson

sleeps soundly, gorged on mother's milk and lulled
by the heat while today's fallen get back up, and I
make my first vow to tell him everything.

The Loa Loa

In memory of my lost money

The loa loa, also known as the eye worm,
jet sets along the banks of the great Congo river,
first class astride the jaws of biting Chrysops,
looking for someone, anyone, to land on

whose pounds of flesh might serve his secret need.
Jaques Cousteau, missionary, native—all the same
to him: a lifelong banquet delivered to his door
in a fine hotel, free for the duration of his stay

should you be rafting, motoring or canoeing
in between limpid and soulful rain forest banks
dreaming, perhaps, of curative new unguents
pulsing through the stems of rare weeds.

You are his luxury ticket and you can count on it—
this savvy little worm knows his way around
and because he was born stupid and made mean
what he does to you isn't personal—no,

it's only business, an all-consuming hunger.
So your path has crossed with his and you are,
in the vernacular, infected. Everything seems all right
but he's in there, working soundlessly inside you,

swimming forward, forward and upward toward
his own brand of manifest destiny—I should say

destination, because he has one, and only one,
via your labrynthian pulmonary system

to that place in you where this world and the other
are tethered to each other, outward to inward,
by the optic nerve, until he feasts there
upon your very sight, now his, and you go blind.

Traveler, beware. Watch for the fugitive swelling
that comes and goes when he first singles you out
because, given enough time, he will become
impossible to remove, except by scalpel.

Telling Stories

That night at the live sex show in Paris
when the tall brunette waded through the aisles and
hoisted up one lean strong leg against yours
in a way that could say nothing else but
remove this silk stocking at once, you
complied as if you belonged in exactly
that red velvet chair in the back row
with me next to you, too amazed
to be embarrassed by anything. It was

only us, a few Japanese tourists,
a woman from Wisconsin who looked as if she'd
this moment been abducted by aliens,
probably as surprised as us by the virtuosity
of what we were seeing, and the "performers,"
whom we later nicknamed Jacques and Vivienne
after the characters in the French textbook
we had studied before flying out of Houston.

It was just after learning you were dying,
where you lay under a cold bag of blood
in a hospital ward already familiar to us both,
that we did what we were best at: planning,
going into near hysterics over what our friends
would say. Every tearful condolence
was to be endured politely, then you'd declare
how you and I were going to Europe. I was vain,

then, about being the other half of your story.
I didn't know that most of the people we impressed
would be dead themselves or stuck
in that manifest process by the time
I could try to remember what we were

to each other. And what were we? We were
nights out that don't bear the telling,
long afternoons of "trashing" a few
select people we knew, and whole weekends
of shopping. We were God and the Devil,
you liked to say after way too many cocktails,
created to tempt one another. During one trip
to Seattle, we saw Wagner's entire *Ring*.
The director passed out twice, was revived twice,
and kept going. "Low blood sugar," was the rumor.
That summer I bought you silk stockings

for your Garden Party outfit. You melted
a record into the shape of a hat
and found a wig that, when turned backwards,
and, blow-dried with tons of Vo5,
looked like Tina Turner's hair. I went

as your date in a rented tuxedo, my hair greased
back, a moustache and beard glued on.
That night a headlight went out on your car.
The handsome policeman who pulled us over
took one look in the window
and told us to go home. The next day

it was back to the phones in the house
of undisclosed location where men,
whose homes and lovers had failed to outlast
the enduring patience of darkness,

came to wait. Sometimes one of them
would show up in the doorway near where
I sat and stand there watching us for minutes,
stock-still and thin as an X-ray negative.

And what did I say to the kid who called
in terror of mosquitoes, whose schoolteacher
had described to him a world of microcosmic

terrrorists, kamikazes in the blood,
or the lady who wouldn't let her kids
go near a pool? Every day
I told a hundred people not to worry. I sang
the virtues of temperance and "safe sex,"
rules I'd memorized from the leaflet
with teddy bears pictured on the front
while you kept your ear glued to another line,
drumming up money, or talking to Leif Lippert,
your lover right out of a Viking movie. He would die
two years before you near his favorite bar
in Key West. If, in the history of the Western World
air ever sizzled, it was when the two of you

danced . . . Anyway, the day after our night
on the Rue de Pigalle, we maneuvered the car
through Paris and out to Chartres to see
the cathedral. Inside, the dark was full
and cold. Even more than the last

night at the Club Lolita, I felt the voyeur.
Your approaching death was *immense,* a vaulted thing
that closed in around us and drove me away
to the one warm corner where the Virgin
sat back in her recess surrounded by tapers
and little old French ladies fingering beads.

By the way, I got all the money to Michael
from the insurance policy you got by lying
on the application. Fuck Prudential:
he deserved it after caring for you
during those last months while you fought
the brain cancer's slow erasure of your personality
by spending every penny he brought home
redecorating your apartment. And it was *flawless,*

a chromatic blue of pastels set off
by Michael's intolerable plants. Nate,
the other night the rock star Prince
was on TV, performing his new hit single
more lubriciously than ever. A clear
vinyl panel was sewn into the back
of his pants so that when he turned
you could see his butt. I missed you

more than ever, hearing your laugh,
then your voice, work it, Mary, so clearly
that for an instant you were here, not
part of any sententious darkness

just the small one friends make, in secret, together.

The James Dickey Contemporary Poetry Series

Edited by Richard Howard

Error and Angels
Maureen Bloomfield

Ripper!
Carl Jay Buchanan

Portrait in a Spoon
James Cummins

From the Bones Out
Marisa de los Santos

The Land of Milk and Honey
Sarah Getty

All Clear
Robert Hahn

Without a Witness
Stella Johnston

A Taxi to the Flame
Vickie Karp

Growing Back
Rika Lesser

Hours of the Cardinal
Richard Lyons

Lilac Cigarette in a Wish Cathedral
Robin Magowan

Traveling in Notions: The Stories of Gordon Penn
Michael J. Rosen

United Artists
S. X. Rosenstock

The Threshold of the New
Henry Sloss

Green
Sidney Wade